About the Author

Alan Murphy was born in Dublin on the last day ... later he received a diploma in fine art after thr... College of Art and Design (as it was then know... ...his paintings in Dublin, Sligo and Belfast and published a handful of poems, mostly in England.

He is currently based in Lismore, Co. Waterford where he lives above a book shop.

First published in Ireland by AvantCard Publications, 2009

All rights reserved

©Copyright 2009 Alan Murphy
Illustrations ©2009 Alan Murphy

A CIP catalogue record for this book is available
from the British Library.

ISBN 978 0 9561734 0 9

*©ADAGP, Paris and DACS, London 2008
Marc Chagall
Paris Through the Window
1913
Oil on canvas
53 1/2 x 55 3/4 inches (135.8 x 141.4cm)
Solomon R. Guggenheim Museum, New York
Solomon R. Guggenheim Founding Collection, By gift
37.438

Printed by Collins Print and Packaging Ltd. Tel: 021 4909160

AvantCard Publications, The Bookshop, Chapel Street,
Lismore, Co. Waterford

Poems
and Illustrations

by

Acknowledgements

Though this little tome has been in the pipeline for quite a while, Corina Duyn is to a large extent responsible for snatching it from the jaws of oblivion. She arranged the book on her computer, took photos and contributed a few ideas to the layout. Hartelijk bedankt. A big thank you also to Declan and Michael of the Irish ME Trust for their generous contribution towards printing costs. Finally cheers to Ronan (and Sha) at Alphabet Soup for much crucial work on those pesky illustrations and the cover. The Artwork is in the post!

Thanks also to the following for help and encouragement: Trish Lewis, Louise (typing), Des (photographs), P J Brady, Brid MacSweeney and Jenni Duggan (proofreaders), Tony Murphy, Deirdre Lillis, Susan Knight, Maeve Friel, the Tyrone Guthrie Centre, the Guggenheim Museum, Inka Design (Lismore), Niall, Anita, Hin, Aidan and Winnie, and young critics, Muireann and Faolán.

The Chagall painting is reproduced by permission of the Design and Artists copyright society (London). The Pauline Kael quotation is from "Is there a cure for film criticism?" in *I Lost it at the Movies* (Marion Boyars 1965).

The first prerogative of an artist in any medium is to make a fool of himself.
                    -Pauline Kael

Contents

The Live Computer	1
The Cheerful Ghost	3
Why 2K?	5
The Alien Binmen	7
Pablo Picasso	9
The Professor of the Non-Serious	11
Hippy Poem	14
Fashion	17
The Devil's Hot Water Bottle	19
Transformations	21
Come Clean	23
The Palace of Sweet Dreams	25
Things	27
An Octopus	29
I'm Bored	32
Once in a Purple Moon	33
Me Too	35
According to Marc Chagall	37
Funk and Jazz	39
Two Santas	41
Off the Top of Me Head	42
The Biggest Kid in the Whole Wide World	43
Crazy Clichés	45
Adventures in Alchemy	47
Obnoxious Ode	50
I Love Hatred	51
Riddle Me This	53
The Mona Lisa's on our Fridge	55
Deep Contentment	58

The Live Computer

We bought it in a high-tech shop,
We took it home and let it drop
In a small boxroom, all quiet and neat.

It sat there on a little table,
We didn't know that it was able,
Being made of circuits, chips and bytes.

But as we were about to leave
We could have sworn we heard it wheeze,
We could have sworn we heard it take a breath.

Then closing round it like a net,
We were surprised to see it fret,
We were surprised to see it start to sweat.

And, with our wonder all a-quiver,
We were confused to see it shiver,
We were alarmed to see it tremble so.

It showed us this was not the half
By letting out a boisterous laugh,
A guffaw no computer ever gave.

And without letting time go by
It next produced an anguished cry,
A howling searing anguished cry.

By this we were perplexed somewhat;
We had not plugged it in its slot,
And yet it seemed to live and breathe and roar.

But when we did it let a sigh,
And of a sudden seemed to die,
And then the live computer was no more.

The Cheerful Ghost

It seems like ages since the cheerful ghost
Came to stay.

He blew in on a Tuesday through a closed front door,
He sleeps on the ceiling and dances on the floor,
He'd howl and moan and bellow but he doesn't know what
It's for;
He's just cheerful.

He likes to giggle whenever he can.
He's also eaten all the jam.

He watches all our videos and sometimes smokes in bed,
He hasn't any limbs or a torso or a head,
Just a disembodied smile that's never been fed.
He's not grumpy.

He goes to bed at eight o'clock.
He's rarely known to jeer or mock.

He feasts in the kitchen and sings in the bath,
He makes hoax phone calls to his buddies for a laugh,
Has to wear a white sheet but he thinks it's daft;
He's just happy.

So if you see him don't despair,
Don't be fearful and don't beware,
He's just sunny and misunderstood,
He's our cheerful ghost.

Why 2k?

An old man hauled a giant object
Across the land.

It was the letter K.

It took him a thousand years.

He hauled it up a hill.
He stopped, wheezing and gasping for breath
At regular intervals.

It *was* made of stone after all.

If he'd lived in Hollywood all would have been fine,
They'd have had a celebration, a toast with some wine...

But there's no K's in Hollywood.
This was Plymouth.

There's no K's in Plymouth either
But that didn't deter him.
He continued out of a sense of spite.

When the K was at the top of the hill
He dragged another one across the land to keep it company.
That also took a thousand years.

So, when he was finished there were two giant K's
On top of a hill in Plymouth.

Later that day it rained a bit.

But who knows? Maybe some day
In the dim and distant future
Those self-same letters will be as famous
As the friendly sunlit letters of Hollywood.

Who knows? Who can tell?

The Alien Binmen

One December day in the failing light
A weird little spaceship lay out of sight
As creatures descended from mars.

It was dark, it was dim, but still clear to see;
These beings meant business, oh aye.

Their skin was all slimy, scaly and green
And their rasping breath was rather obscene;
An alien's breath, oh aye.

They came one by one 'til their number was big
And danced as they worked a strange alien jig,
The alien binmen, oh yes.

Monsters as far as the eye can see
Collecting the rubbish for you and for me,
'cause gold's no good to them.

Extra-terrestrials defying all facts,
Slinging our refuse up on their backs,
Oh yes.

And when they were finished they took it away,
From street to spaceship in a luminous ray,
And then disappeared in a cloud of pale light,
The type that would give your granny a fright.

Nobody knows why they did it.
Nobody knows where they hid it.
But one thing's for sure, they're coming back,
'cause junk is their jewellery and full was their sack.

Pablo Picasso

Pablo Picasso
Was balding a bit
But that didn't stop him
From loving the ladies.

His paint brush was fluent,
His feet they were fine
And dancing with women
Was like drinking wine.

He loved to paint them,
He loved to kiss them,
But most of all
He loved to miss them.

Pablo Picasso
Was balding a lot
But that didn't stop him
From falling in love.

Though he walked with a cane
He continued to paint
And loved with a passion,
And still found it quaint.

And when he was old
And fit for his bed,
He got his new girlfriend
To warm it instead!

And when he was lying
In eternal rest
The grandest of tombstones
Lay on his chest.

The Professor of the Non-serious

The professor of the non-serious
Has a pair of windscreen-wiper spectacles
On the end of his nose.
He reads lots of big important books,
Each page of which is painted a different colour.
One half of his suit is tweed, the other pinstripe.
His entire family is made out of cheese.

The professor of the non-serious
Delivers lectures in his bathtub.
When the holidays come he eats his ruler.
He has a car that runs on orange juice.
And a bicycle that runs on the moon.
Instead of buying pets he moved into a zoo.
And always turns out the light before sneezing.
He drinks cocoa from a teapot each night
Before going to bed.
And he has a wife who doesn't understand him.

The professor of the non-serious
Has a degree in gibberish.
And a PHD in perversity.
He plays football with his elbows.
And uses a chair for table tennis.
He likes to watch the sun go down by telephone.
And he has a guitar that has all its strings, but no guitar.

Thus his life in every respect is decidedly eccentric;
His study is on wheels,
              And he munches marbles between meals.
He sometimes has a cat,
              But more often a tiger, a flea or a bat.

The professor of the non-serious doesn't think it's funny.
His socks have started communicating with extra-terrestrials.
His front lawn has turned a subtle shade of purple.
And his house has started to dance.

The professor of the non-serious is studying mankind.
He's sure that someone has made a mistake.
He tries to remedy the situation
              Every moment that he is awake.

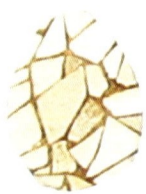

Hippy Poem

Hey,
Did ye know
You can see a flower grow?
Hey, did ye know
You can do it?
You can catch it before the wind blew it.
You can film it before the world knows.

Hey,
Did ye know
You can see a plant live?
Hey, did ye know
You can do it?
You can stand in the garden and woo it.
You can watch its green fingers unfold.

From tiniest seed
To leafy abundance;
It's labours and efforts
Before it's redundance.
Did you know that it can be quite trippy?
Especially if you're a hippy!

And did you know
If you look at a rose
You can see the face of desire?
And it starts when the world is on fire.
It's patently, obviously so.

Though flowers might be soppy, girly and sad,
They are sometimes delirious, fiercesome and mad,
And herbal tea drinkers had better beware
That those delicate petals are also a snare
To trap the incendiary sun.
D'you want to see how it's done?

Hey,
Did ye know
You can see a flower grow?
Hey, did ye know
You can do it?
You can catch it before the wind blew it.
You can film it before the world knows.

Fashion

Punk rock was a-pulsing in seventy-seven,
But now all the Mohawks have gone straight to heaven.

Men's make-up was in for the eighties as well,
But's nowadays deemed to be desperately *unswell*.

And what ever happened to Elvis's quiff?
Did somebody turf it off of a cliff?
Nobody, nobody knows...

Remember those jeans with legs wide as a tent,
When skin-tight threads, glitter and glam were the bent?
Then there were safety pins, acne and boots;
Heads sprouting colourful, dangerous shoots.
Strangely, so strangely alive...

Suppose a hip alien blew in from space;
What would he make of the humanoid race?
What would he put on, what clothes and what wig?
Which fifteen minutes of fad would he dig?
Trendy, so trendy he'd seem...

Fashions that came and went like a comet;
The posing, the sneering, the tunes and the vomit!
Passions that flared and burnt out in due course;
Groupies that screamed and yelled 'til they were hoarse.
Weirdly, so weirdly passé...

And what's going to happen in future instead,
To bury the past, every stitch, every thread?
Will we wear space-age clothes custom made
                              for the air,
  And dangle new jewellery exotic and rare?
  Or will we continue to reference the past?
That Stone Age of style that we're free from
                              at last!

The Devil's Hot Water Bottle

The devil slid down the banisters,
He was almost ready for bed,
He fumed with fallen angel's glee;
Beady little eyes in a beady little head,
Baby horns already there,
Telltale hoof prints on the stair,
A tail to swish with coy restraint,
A conscience very very faint,
A trainee's trident by his side
And
Of course
His hot water bottle.

The devil's hot water bottle!
It was very very hot.
Hotter than Beelzebub's brain,
Hotter than a fuming train,
Hotter than an African plain,
So hot.

It was even hotter than lava floods,
Hotter than some stolen goods,
Hotter than the burning woods,
That hot.

He tucked it under angelic sheets
And had himself a supper snack
And rested for awhile without a care.
He'd mucked about
And played some tricks
On gods and giddy kings,
Hyper in his diaper since
God told him to get to bed.

And finally he got in bed
And as he lay his fire went out,
And his boiling bottle soon became,
With the passing of time, tepid and tame;
He clutched it gingerly with delicate fingers
And dreamed a little of heaven.

He'd fooled around
And knocked the world
A little off it's course,
Jumpin' in his jammies since
God told him to get to bed.

He'd played the prince
And mocked the law
Of grown-ups and godheads,
Hyper in his diaper since
God told him to get to bed!

Transformations

I went for a swim
And turned into a fish;
Some day I might just wind up on your dish.

I jumped in the air
And turned into a bird.
If I told how it happened you'd think it absurd.

I went for a walk
And I never came back,
And that's about all I can say...

The sea was so blue as it sparkled and swam,
Surrounding and swallowing all that I am.

The sky was so vast that it went on for miles,
Bearing and buffeting me.

And as for the walk, well that gave me a fit!
That was the really interesting bit;

As I strolled a great hurricane blew me away,
Right into outer space for the day.

This treacherous tempest put me down soon,
And left me to finish my walk on the moon!

Come Clean

When you blotted your copybook leaving a stain - come clean.
When you left a dog howling out in the rain - come clean.
When you shivered in shadows and ran down that lane - come clean.

When you threw a great diamond into the sea - come clean.
When you ran off from school 'cause they charged quite a fee - come clean.
When you thought you were Superman when you were three - come clean.

When you tried to bake cakes but it ended in tears - come clean.
When you forgot to wash behind your ears - come clean.
When you fell off your bike ending up on your rear - come clean.

When you thought that a girl's name was April showers - come clean.
When you tasted some milk and you thought it was sour - come clean.
When you've been for a bath and you've soaked there awhile - come clean.

The Place of Sweet Dreams

I asked a glow-worm where dreams come from
In a curious whispered hiss;
It paused a moment to reflect
And told me dreams are this:

*God's own private purple thoughts
All wrapped up in crazy paper
Sent on down to
Merest Mortals
His own hand-chosen
Dearest Mortals
All stumbling and snoring
In a world of deep slumber
All mumbling and pouring with sweat
Not as yet
Free to stop themselves soaring
Through fever and falling!*

I asked a firefly 'bout our dreams,
It paused in deep thought for awhile
And after much consideration
Answered in this style:

Dreams are mind sculpture
Stored up in big boxes
And moved onto tired-eyed ships of sleep
Which sail to a lullaby land
Of nod
Where the tired dreamer plods
In boots made of burdened brass
No horse and no mule and no ass
To lighten his lazy-head load.

I asked the bright bug one more question;
Why are dreams so weird?
It said to me quite cheerfully
The answer's in God's beard!

He let it grow some time ago
It grew and grew in mortals' minds
It wrapped them up for sleepy night
In a freaky place that's out of sight:
The palace of Sweet Dreams.

I thanked the insect for its insights,
Mulled them over in my head
And just to test its wacky theories
Went off home and went to bed!

Things

Kids are smaller than carnivals,
Bicycles bigger than beards,
Rats are longer than grains of rice
And insects are just plain weird.

Toast is lighter than tons of gold,
Pigs are fatter than most,
Parties are full or incredibly dull
Depending on who is the host.

Cakes are more sweet than cathedrals,
As boats are much wetter than birds,
Soft cheese is elasticy,
Raincoats are plasticy,
And of owls I shall not say a word.

Doors swing ajar when you push them
But stones stay incredibly still,
Oceans are large, teachers in charge
But the wild wind has its own will.

An Octopus

An octopus floating under the sea,
Perfectly happy, perfectly free,
Wading and wandering under the sea,
Well where the hell else would it be?

Under a table, under the sink?
That would be slightly absurd don't ye think?
No, an octopus floats about under the sea,
Perfectly happy to be.

A jellyfish floating under the sea,
Perfectly frivolous, perfectly free,
No job to go to, no daily grind,
No brains, no bones and no body you'll find,
Just a jellyfish heart and a jellyfish mind,
Perfectly happy to be.

And when you're in school
And you're doing your sums,
You can count all these creatures
On fingers and thumbs;
You can count them all day
But they won't count you back,
For all knowledge of human endeavours they lack,
And that's why they dropped out a long time ago
In an ocean so vast that its size you can't know,
Perfectly frivolous, perfectly fabulous,
Perfectly happy to be.

Think of each day just the same as the last;
Octopus future as octopus past,
Roaming and rambling under the waves,
Think of it and you will see.

And think of the day when you get a degree;
When the lessons accumulate 'til you are free,
You can jump in the ocean just one more time
And search its blue depths for a song or a rhyme,
Sounding the octopus.

I'm Bored

Want to climb up the Eiffel tower - I'm bored.
Want to talk for hours and hours - I'm bored.
Want to jump in a lake of lava - I'm bored.
Want to grow my own giant banana - I'm BORED AS HELL.

Want to go swimming with mermaids and merqueens - I'm yawning.
Want to kick the sun into the cosmos - it's dawning.
Want to explode with ideas and life - I'm restless.
Want to unload all my sorrows and strife - I'm breathless.

Want to paint paintings to hang in the Louvre - Life's tedious.
Want them to nod and to wink and to move - What genius.
Want to float peacefully into oblivion - Time's a drag.
Want all the grown-ups to turn into little uns - No more Dads.

Want to go jogging on the moon - I'm bored.
Think I'll be six feet under quite soon - I'm bored bored bored.
Want to find interesting pastimes to play - I'm bored by ten.
Guess I'll just have to make up more fun things - Until then.

Once in a Purple Moon

Once in a purple moon
The cat sails a balloon
Into the heart of an apple tart
Whilst merrily singing a tune.

Once in a purple moon
The garden starts to dance,
The flowers all float to a quirky note
Of music, as in a trance.

Every lilac year
A badger bends my ear;
Half filled with ale, he tells me a tale
That's full of friendly cheer.

Once in a purple moon
You can see it snowing in June;
The sun cracks in two, then turns to goo
And it's due to happen quite soon.

Once in a purple moon
The motorway starts to rise,
It sends all the cars on a trip to mars,
You can witness it if you're wise.

Every lilac year
On a day that's grey and drear,
The sun comes out and starts to shout,
It's a wonderful thing to hear!

Me Too

Have you ever had a dream that was crazy?
Have you ever had a dog that was lazy?
Have you ever had a thought that was just a bit hazy?
Funnily enough, me too.

Have you ever ate a dish that's Italian?
Have you ever seen a horse that's a stallion
Run like the wind and then drink a gallion?
That's a funny thing - Me too.

Have you ever picked a flower that was perfumed?
Or watched a whole hour that was costumed
At home on the telly at nine o'clock?
Isn't that a gas - Me too.

Have you ever dodged a fist that was angry?
Or lodged a lover's kiss that was manly?
Went on a summery trip with your family?
Isn't that amazing - Me too.

And have you had a goldfish that shimmered?
Or glimpsed a pile of money that glimmered?
But once out of reach became dimmer and dimmer?
Tell me something new - Me too.

Have you baked bread that came out all knobbly?
Devoured a dessert that was wobbly?
Stole all these similar scenes right off me?
Let me say to you - Me. too.

According to Marc Chagall
(Marc Chagall, Modern Painter 1887 - 1985)

How does it rain if the rain rains upwards?
-in the mind of Marc Chagall.
How can a bun turn into the sun?
-by the power of Marc Chagall.
And when does a town recline on a cloud?
-when its world is Marc Chagall's.

Look how the goat gets the vote
In the pictures of Marc Chagall.
And how the fiddler starts to float
In the daydreams of Marc Chagall.
And, oh, how gravity wanes and withers
According to Marc Chagall.

The dumbest animals start to talk
To incredulous faces which turn and gawp
As the Eiffel tower starts to walk,
Following Marc Chagall.

So doff your hat but hold on to your head;
Just lose your logical limits instead,
And gamely greet green, orange and red
-the music of Marc Chagall.

"Paris through the window" by Chagall *

Funk and Jazz

It comes out of the radio.
It's called Funk.
It's music but what is it made of?

Funk is a rubber band wrapped round a bed spring.
Funk is flowing and foolish, dripping and easy.
Funk is all curves and splashes.
Funk can't be canned, it swims in the sea.
D'you see?

It rolls out of the radio.
It's called jazz.
It's music but what is it made of?

Jazz is a packet of effervescence.
Jazz is a long slide at the end of the day.
Jazz accelerates the soul.
Jazz is the drums of Africa, the bugels of New York.
Hark, hark.

And what happens when the two become one?
Jazzy Funk,
Funky Jazz,
Delirious dynamite,
Groovy gold,
A wild and explosive mixture I'm told.

If it all gets too much here's what to do:
Plug up your ears and shut your eyes,
Say nothing and creep away
And live to be blinded another day.

Two Santas

Christmas is coming, the goose is quite plump
But ole Daddy Christmas has got the hump;
From north pole to south and from east unto west
All kids make demands that won't give him a rest!

The burden of being bestower of gifts
Is too much for one overworked grandad to lift,
Reindeer and helpers are just not enough,
Two santas are needed to do all the work!

Off the Top of Me Head

Off the top of me head
A river of reason bled,
Filling up every
Cranny and crook
With wisdom wine instead.

Off the top of me head
I thought up something good;
In the wink of an eye
Which was no longer dry
The idea became a flood.

Off the top of me crown
The truth came tumbling down;
A man's name, his address,
His wife with a dress
All skittered to the ground.

The Biggest Kid in the Whole Wide World

My face is bigger than space itself
And my cheeks are warmed by cosmic suns;
My eyes are diamonds that see in the dark
And my ears can hear the planets dance.

My neck is ninety-nine miles long;
It sways in the stratosphere, nothing wrong.
Birds are aghast and pilots agog;
A thirteen-year old looming out of the fog.

I've wrapped my body around the earth;
Where my boots leave off my shoulders start.
I've eight million addresses, haven't you heard?
I'm the biggest kid in the whole wide world.

Crazy Clichés

Its raining cats and deer today
And eggs are moony side up
Cause all the clichés that exist
Have gotten all mixed up!

The phrases that we know have fled,
We've searched from here to Lapland
But spotting an honest-to-goodness one
Is like finding a needle in a hatstand!

Language that was sure as stone
Has collapsed like a house of cads,
Now we've all got our tyres crossed,
Our brogue is barking mad!

It's enough to make you tear your tongue out,
It beatifies belief,
You just can't find a well-worn saying
For love nor money nor grief.

I've called off the whole search at last,
Thrown in the owl, given up the toast,
I'm resting on my lapels now,
Clutching a faithful hope;

That one fine hour the sun may rise
On a new day that's devoid
Of mangled and confuséd words
That get all folk annoyed.

Until that day I'll bide my tomb
And wait with bated brat,
Calmly keeping my fungus crossed
For a goodbye to all that!

Adventures in Alchemy

Show me a simpleton and I'll show you a sage.
Show me lean times and I'll show you a wage.
Show me an ape and I'll show you a god.
Show me your plate and I'll fill it with cod.

Show me fool's dirt and I'll show you fine gold.
Show me an egg and I'll show you the old.
Show me grim facts and I'll show you great myths.
Show me some wood and I'll chop it to bits.

Show me a stain and I'll show you a sheen.
Show me a thing and I'll show you a being.
Show me a hole and I'll show you a well.
Give me a kiss and I swear I won't tell.

Show me a cad and I'll show you a king.
Show me the blues and I'll show you the bling.
Show me the start and I'll show you the end.
Show me a foe and I'll show you a friend.

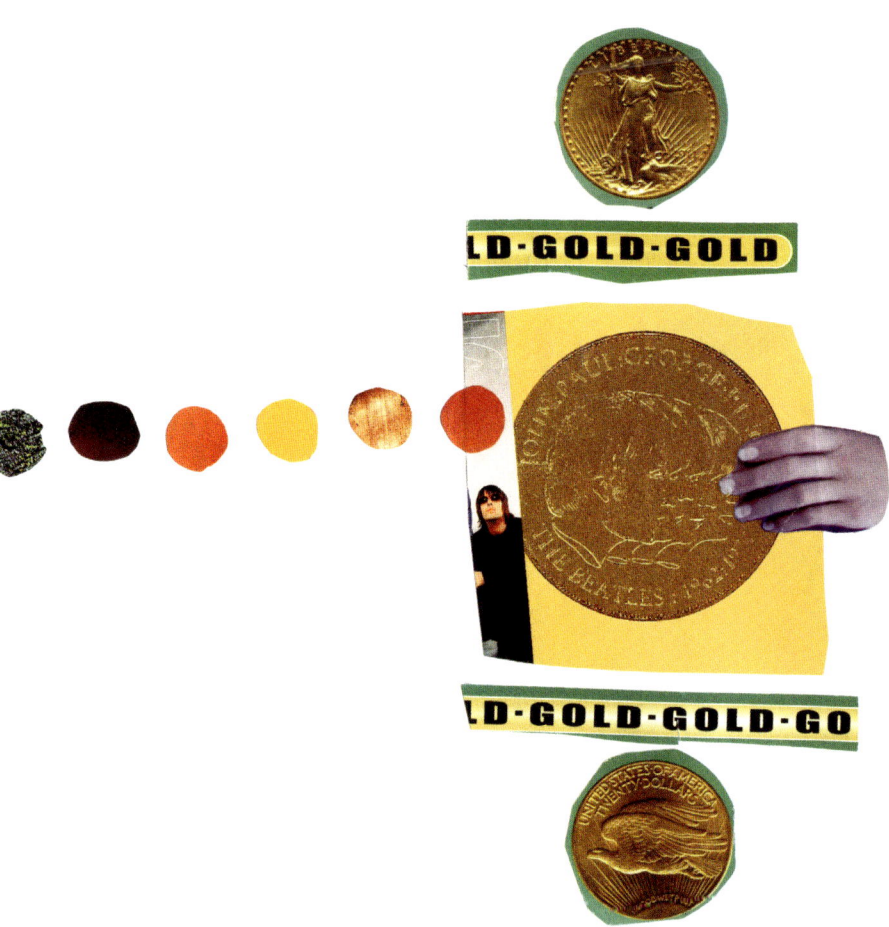

Obnoxious Ode

I wandered lonely as a crowd,
In hobnail boots went stomping round,
And filled the air with a hue and cry
That frightened lots of passers-by.

I rested peaceful as a din;
The sun saw me and it went in,
I drank some cans of beer as well;
'twas then my voice began to swell:

I sang as tuneful as a brute;
No-one accompanied me on flute,
The wind's reply was all I heard;
I don't think it believed a word.

I wandered lonely as a crowd,
The trees looked on with furrowed brows,
The birds aghast dropped from their nests
To see this rowdy rustic pest!

I love hatred,
I strip off in the cold,
I eat asparagus for kicks;
I prefer rust to gold.

I like faulty technology
And bands that are well out-of-date,
I'm breezy, alert and wide-eyed in discussions
On tragedy, death and fate.

Staying in is adventurous,
Going out is for freaks.
Once when a bully gave me a bruise
I smiled for several weeks.

ABBA the loudest band in the world,
Hairdressers dangerous thugs,
I decorate my bedroom with paintings of
Rats and spiders and bugs.

Watch me, I'll grin in a maths class
And frown when at last we're set free.
Standing still in a playground chase
Ensures that you can't catch me.

I like liking
Things that everyone hates.
Touch me, I'm real;
It's part of the deal.
Go off and tell all your mates.

Riddle Me This

How long is a piece of string?
How wide is a patch of earth?
How deep is a grave dug by a knave?
As long as a rattlesnake's grin.

How close is a near thing?
How far is a ferry's spume
When it reaches the sand of a distant land?
As close as a Christmas king.

How old is the oldest hill?
How young is a baby's cheek?
Put them together, they make strange weather.
As old as the world's will.

The Mona Lisa's on our Fridge

The Mona Lisa's on our fridge,
Wearing a sort of smile,
But we've a confession, the artist's impression
Is wide of the mark by a mile!

Her eyes are like two pan-fried eggs
In a silly sea of pink;
Her nose and mouth all inside out,
One loony squiggle of ink.

Her hair's a crazy hurricane
Of scribbles all around
A splodgy face that's lost all grace
And looks a bit unsound.

She looks like she's had a couple of beers.
Get a load of those ears!

Her body has seen better days
And's all a bit confused;
Her boobs are backwards, her bottom's bent,
She's battered, broke and bruised!

Don't fall for her charms.
She has too many arms!

Suffice to say that no one paid
A dime to see this dame.
We charged a fee for her to see
But (sadly) no one came.

The Mona Lisa's on our fridge,
A masterpiece of mush,
But now it's time to make a change
In time for the gold rush.

The Mona Lisa's on our fridge,
It's time to take her off,
Replace her with some sunflowers
By a toddler called Van Gogh.

Deep Contentment.

I dived in an ocean called Deep Contentment,
Swam at the surface and watched all the waves,
Then I dived deeper and deeper and deeper,
Thought I was diving for days.

I met a blue whale there called Calm Enchantment,
A glorious sleepy-eyed monstrous sage;
He took out his pipe and he told me his life;
All eight thousand years of his age.

I found out the colour of Deep Contentment,
Found that its hue was inside of my head;
So I left the deep to its watery sleep
And swam back up to the city.

AUTHOR'S NOTE: Although there have in recent years been many sightings of the alien binmen, few people have emerged unscathed by the experience. If you have a visit from these sinister workmen, rest assured that they are NOT a figment of your imagination and that YOU ARE NOT ALONE. On the other hand, if you tell anyone about these experiences, you may appear to be a fuzzy individual who has lost one or two of his marbles.